LITTLE CHIDAMBARA

SUNIL M AND CHINMAYEE KATTI

This book is dedicated to Param Poojya Marthand Dixitaru, a true Saint whose wisdom has illuminated the path to oneness. His unwavering realization of Brahman has inspired countless seekers on their journey toward discovering the truth of the self and the universe.

With your divine blessings, may this book serve as a stepping stone for all the curious young minds who ponder the mysteries of the world and ask life's profound questions.

With gratitude,
Gangadhar Dixit
Hubli, Karnataka

Contents

CHAPTER ONE

Akasha Chidambara Kshetra

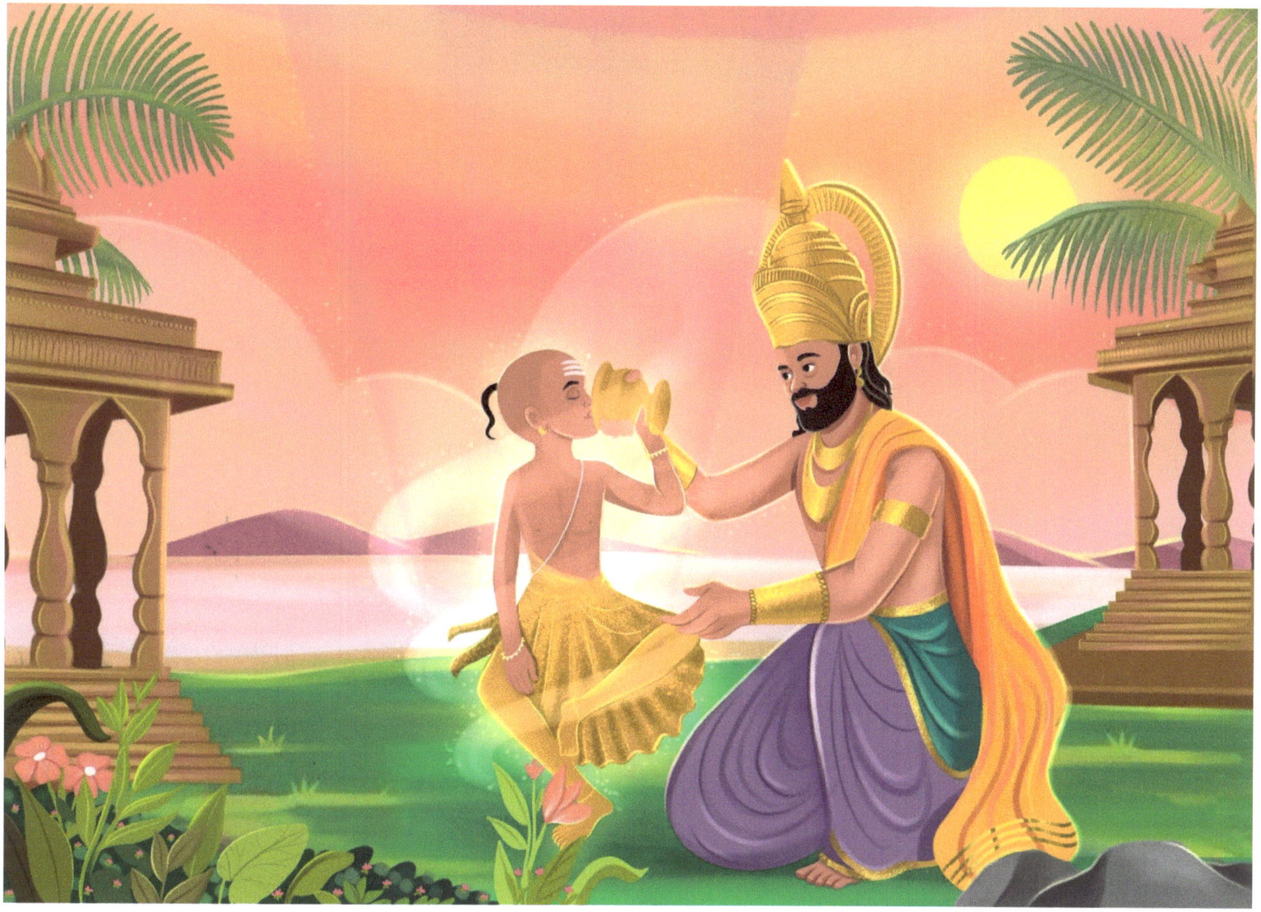

Once upon a time, there was a king named Prithvipati who was very sick. He had a skin disease called leprosy that made him feel very unwell. No matter what doctors did, he couldn't get better. The king felt very sad and tired of being sick. One day, while he was sitting near a pool, a curious event happened. A wild boar came and jumped into the pool. When it came out, its skin looked shiny and golden!

The king was amazed and curious about what happened. So, he decided to dip himself into the pool too. And guess what? All his sickness was cured, and his skin turned golden too! That's when he realized that there was something magical about that pool.

The king decided to look around the pool and found five temples hidden under the sand. But these temples didn't have any statues of gods inside them. So, the king thought of making golden statues to put in those temples. But every time he tried; the golden statues would break.

One day, an old man came to the king and told him something wise. He said that while making the golden statues, a young Brahmin boy would come and ask for food. If the king did what the boy asked, then the statues would be successful.

So, the king tried again. And just as the old man said, a young boy came and asked for food. The king was puzzled, but he did what the boy asked. He poured the liquid gold into the boy's mouth, and suddenly, the boy turned into a beautiful statue of Lord Nataraja, the god of dance!

The king was so happy and installed the statue in one of the temples. Today, this place is known as Akasha Chidambara. And in the main temple, you can still see the golden statue of Lord Nataraja dancing happily!

The Boon of Chidambara

There was a very wise man named Marthanda Dixit and his wife. They went to this place Akasha Chidambara and prayed to God for 12 whole years! Every single day, they offered a juice to God made from Bermuda grass, and they only took this as their own food for 12 years. One night, while Marthanda Dixit was asleep, he had a dream. In his dream, God Shiva appeared and asked if he wanted any boon. Marthanda Dixit asked for a son just like God Shiva. Amazingly, God promised to be born as their son! God even gave Marthanda Dixit the signs to know it was really Him. He said there would be certain marks on the baby's ear, and the baby would be like an 8-year-old kid when born. Marthanda Dixit was so happy when he woke up! He told his wife about the dream, and they finished their prayers happily. Then they went back to their home feeling very blessed.

CHAPTER THREE

Birth of Chidambara

Marthanda Dixit and Sadhvi Lakshmi went back home to Muragodu a remote village in Karnataka, they continued doing their prayers and rituals. While Sadhvi Lakshmi was pregnant, she spent lots of time meditating and praying to Chidambara. She talked about wise and spiritual things from ancient books. Marthanda Dixit was very happy about her and even arranged for a baby shower ceremony to celebrate the upcoming baby.

After nine months, on November 20, 1758, a Monday, A baby boy was born, and it was a special day called Kartika Shashti according to Hindu calendar. When the baby was born, the room was filled with bright light, and the baby himself shone as bright as the sun! There was a tiny leaf called Bilva in his right ear, and he had special marks on his forehead and hands. Everyone could see that he was something supernatural.

Marthanda Dixit and Sadhvi Laxmi knew right away that this baby was a special incarnation of Lord Chidambara, just like they had prayed for. They were so happy and bowed down to the baby to ask for his blessings. The baby smiled and told them not to worry because all their wishes would come true.

Lots of wise people came to see the baby, and they said that the baby had been born at the auspicious time and place according to the stars. They said he would grow up to be a great Guru (teacher) for everyone. Marthanda Dixit and Sadhvi Lakshmi were so proud! They decided to name the baby "Chidambara" to honour the special place where they had prayed for him. And from that day on, everyone knew that little Chidambara was a special boy, just like a god!

Bala Leela of Chidambara

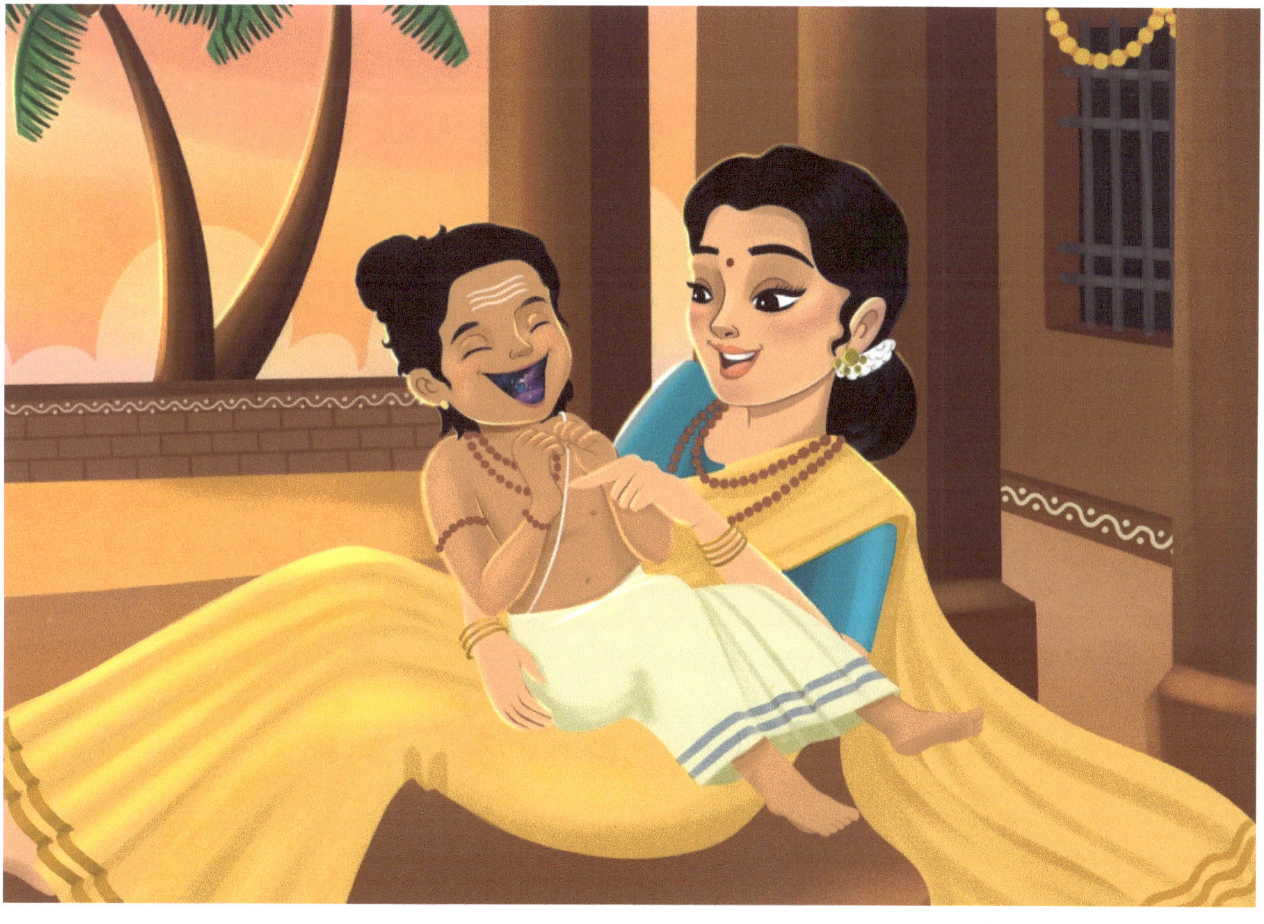

When Chidambara was just a little kid, he loved to play and explore in and around the house. He would sometimes make a lot of a mess, but his mom didn't mind because she enjoyed watching him have fun. Chidambara grew up fast, and he did some amazing things that made everyone amazed.

Once, when Chidambara was eating, he kept his mouth closed tight. His mom had to make him open his mouth, and when she did, she saw something incredible! She saw the whole universe inside his mouth, and she even saw herself feeding him like he was a little god. She was so surprised and told Chidambara's father about it. He said, "Wow, our son really is like a little god!"

Chidambara loved to play with the other kids in the neighbourhood. One day, he built a tiny temple out of some old stuff he found lying around. He put a little pebble inside as the god, and he pretended to offer food and flowers to it. When he gave the other kids some of the soil as a special treat, something magical happened! The soil turned into sweet sugar, the rocks turned into yummy sweets, and the pebble looked just like a real god statue. Everyone was amazed!

Chidambara's dad knew he was a special kid, so he called him and said, "You're really a blessed child, but be careful not to show off too much. It could bring some trouble." Chidambara agreed, but he still did some amazing things almost every day!

After a few years, Chidambara's dad had two more kids, a boy named Prabhakar and a girl named Shesha. They all grew up smart, and their dad taught them important things when they were old enough. They were all special kids, just like Chidambara.

CHAPTER FIVE

Gaja Gouri Vruta

Chidambara was a great helper to his parents, especially during their daily rituals and prayers. He always made sure everything they needed for pooja, like flowers, incense, and lamps, was ready.

One day, a man named Raya came from a nearby village called Hosur to ask Chidambara's dad to do a special ritual called Gaja Gowri Vrata at his home. This ritual was very important because it was said to bring good luck and blessings to kids, just like in the stories of Gandhari and Kunti from the Mahabharata.

Chidambara's dad was busy that day, so he sent Chidambara to help Raya with the ritual. When they got to Raya's house, some of the women there made fun of Chidambara. They didn't think he could help with the ritual because he was just a kid. But Raya knew better and told them that Chidambara was special.

While the women laughed, Chidambara quietly set up the idol of an elephant, which was part of the ritual. Suddenly, the idol came to life and started moving! Chidambara asked the elephant to stay calm and finished all the rituals before having dinner.

After Chidambara left, the elephant idol sprung into life and started going crazy, breaking things in the house. Everyone thought it was because they had made fun of Chidambara. So, they begged him to come back and tame it. Chidambara returned and did a special ritual to calm the elephant down, and it turned back into a regular idol.

Everyone realized that Chidambara was truly special, and they respected him a lot after that.